BELVOIR CASTLE Photo: Christine Matthews

Message from Emma, Duchess of Rutland,
Patron of Dayglo Books Ltd.

   I am delighted to be the patron of Dayglo Books
Ltd. As a person with dyslexia myself, I appreciate
these books being available.

   The people at Dayglo Books have a real passion
for making reading more accessible than ever before
to dyslexic people. They have foresight and talent
and truly believe in the joy of reading for pleasure.

I Have 2 Dog Collars

Revd. Canon

Barbara Holbrook

Published by
Dayglo Books Ltd, Nottingham, UK
www.dayglobooks.co.uk
ISBN 978-1-912256-52-5

Cover photograph by Victoria White
www.darkroomanddigital.co.uk
Cover artwork & illustrations by
www.valentineart.co.uk
Typeset in Opendyslexic
by Abelardo Gonzales (2014)

Printed in England
Distributed by Filament Publishing Ltd

A Message from the Author

In 2004, two things happened that changed my life.

Firstly, I was ordained and became a 'Reverend'. That meant moving from the fast paced and pressured world of IT and business to the emotionally charged and relentless life of church ministry.

Secondly, a small bundle of fun – my first guide dog puppy – came into my life.

Both these events were the start of a new journey of joys and sorrows, making new friends and facing new challenges.

In both cases my dream was, and still is, to change the lives of others for the better.

This book is a chance to share some of the story that brought me here.

Revd. Canon Barbara Holbrook

October 2017

Terminology

The Church of England has a large number of its own words and phrases which may not be familiar to you if you are not a regular member of a Church of England congregation.

On page 103, towards the back of this book, there is a glossary which sets out many of these terms in alphabetical order and explains their meanings.

You may find this helpful to refer to as you are reading.

I Have
2 Dog Collars

Chapter 1

I've been lucky enough to have had
a succession of guide dog puppies in my life over
the past 13 years as a "puppy walker". I wouldn't be
without one. In fact, I'd be lost without one.

To be honest, I think my parish of Kimberley
and Nuthall would be lost without one. My dog has
become a kind of trade-mark thing.

After my previous dog, there was a gap before
my latest puppy arrived. When I started to walk
around with him, you could almost hear the collective
sigh of relief in the parish as things got back to
normal.

People said: "Ah, that's better. It didn't seem
right, you without a dog."

The less stressful you can make life for the puppies, the better. You want to give the puppies every chance to become a guide dog.

There will always be a proportion of puppies that turn out not to be suitable as guide dogs, but you want to make sure that the ones that are suitable don't fall by the wayside for any reason. You want to give each puppy every chance to reach its potential.

Also, you want to identify the ones that aren't going to make it as early in the process as possible, so they can enjoy the life they should be having.

That's partly because it's better for the puppy. If it isn't going to become a guide dog, why put it through all that training? If he's going to be trained for something else, the quicker he gets on to that, the better.

I had one dog who was lovely, very intelligent, very able. You could show him three toys and tell him which one to fetch and he'd pick it out. He could even open all the doors.

But he would never walk in front. As soon as we walked out of that door he followed me.

I said on day one: "He's too good." He was the perfect puppy. Within three days he had learned to sit, wait, stay, come. He would walk nicely on the lead next to me but he would never walk ahead of me.

So he was never going to guide. But as a buddy dog for an autistic child, he was spot on.

There can always be career changes. They could be assistance dogs, they could be police dogs, they could be buddy dogs.

The Guide Dogs charity does actually place some of them with young people with vision impairment so that they can get used to having a dog, to help them to that transition to a guide dog.

Because they are effectively support dogs, they can go to a lot of places that guide dogs can go, although they are not actually guiding the child. They support the child and give them the confidence to be out and about. Since incorporating the Blind Children's Society, Guide Dogs has extended its work with children and young people.

Some of the dogs who don't make it go to be family pets. A lot of people who have these dogs, or retired guide dogs, qualify them as "Pets as Therapy" – or PAT dogs – because the dogs have the right temperament.

We were in a local care home the other day and I bumped into somebody who is also a puppy walker. He owns a dog that was withdrawn from further training and he kept it as a pet. And it was there in the care home as a PAT dog.

They are usually very successful as family pets. If you don't want to get a rescue dog, you could get a dog that for some reason didn't make it as a guide dog, or has retired.

One great advantage is that you will be told the dog's problems. There are not going to be any surprises. You're not going to suddenly find it's got an aversion to blue cars because of something that happened to it in its childhood, or anything else like that.

And it has been thoroughly socialised, so it will be well behaved as a family pet.

Not all the puppies I have walked have gone on to become guide dogs, but they have all been a joy to have in my home.

As I said, I wouldn't be without one.

Dog No. 1

Harvey   October 2004

Harvey was my first puppy. I hadn't realised just what lengths he would go to for food. He managed to break into the cupboard where his food was stored. I was alerted by the munching noise.

I attended a community carol service with a two-month-old puppy so full he could only lie on his back.

He was puppy-shaped down to the bottom of his ribcage, then it was all stomach. You could almost see the outline of some of the kibble.

Harvey

Chapter 2

I do manage to pack a lot in to my days. Sometimes I think my life is quite chaotic, but everything gets done. And believe me, a lot gets done in my parish.

In a year I take more than 200 services, I write and preach 100 sermons, I conduct around 50 funerals, perform 15 to 20 baptisms and solemnise a similar number of weddings.

I participate in more than 100 routine church meetings, as well as dealing with any unexpected urgent matters that crop up. I go to speak to groups of adults and school children.

I keep in touch with fellow priests and try to be

aware of what is going on in other parishes. There is never a dull day.

This morning, for example, I got up and I didn't get a shower until half past eight. I wrote the news sheet. I proofread the church magazine. I finished a presentation on PowerPoint. I put two flyers together and emailed them all to the people who do the photocopying and the person who puts them on the website – all before half past seven! I wouldn't say that is particularly well organised but it had to be done. And it was done.

There's a great variety in my work. I do know how to use my time effectively. It's a learned skill but it's also a habit. And I know how to prioritise.

I can't do everything myself. There are some things only I can do, so they have to be my priority.

I know people have found it difficult knowing that there are a lot of housebound people I haven't been to see. But we have some lovely people who do go and see them.

Luckily, we have members within our congregations who distribute communion at home to housebound people on a monthly basis.

There are many people in the local church community who take on jobs which would just not be done if it was down to me alone to do them.

These are the people who keep the church premises clean and tidy and make sure they are always welcoming with flowers and refreshments.

They run Messy Church, bible studies, Mothers' Union, tea club, and the like. They organise summer fetes and Christmas bazaars. They arrange the lettings for the church halls. They do the multitude of things that go on in a parish which seem to look after themselves, but are in fact done by a very devoted team of volunteers.

With so much activity going on, another skill for me to learn has been the art of apparently 'doing nothing'. Sitting having coffee and chatting to people is part of what I do.

I try to find time to spend just 'being' with people. It's quite hard, because even when I'm just 'being', I'm still the rector.

Many of my congregation can walk round the supermarket and that's simply people walking round the supermarket. I walk round the supermarket and 'the church' has been there.

I go into school and 'the church' has been there. So there are things I can do, just by being there, which other people can't do.

Delegation is an important skill too. My experience in business has taught me that.

I look at people doing things and think:

"I could do that faster."

But if I did, then there would be other things I wouldn't be doing. And they would never learn how to do it.

At work I learned a hard lesson in managing teams, but it pays dividends. Now I will always try to invest in helping people to use their gifts, rather than saying:

"Give that to me, I could do that quicker."

That's how we grow as a church.

If the only things we do are the things I do, it's not much of a community, is it?

It's very simple. We are the body of Christ – the Bible says so – which means everybody has to play their part.

And encouraging people to use their potential is always a valuable thing to do.

I believe that we are made in God's image and that God's will for us is that we should be the best people we can be.

So a lot of the things that we should be doing

in church are good practices everywhere. Because they are about people being fulfilled and achieving their potential.

Dog No. 2

Punch   October 2005

Punch was notorious for just stopping. Halfway across a zebra crossing he would just sit down.

Our puppy walking supervisor asked if there were any issues, and I mentioned this. She asked what I normally did when he stopped, and I said that I just dragged him.

We went out so that she could show me some techniques to get him moving.

After ten minutes, she handed me back the lead and said: "Keep dragging!"

Punch

Chapter 3

In a way, we are victims of our own success.

Some of the people in our congregations find a place in church which they struggle to find in wider society.

What can happen, if you haven't got the right leadership, is that a person stops serving God and starts serving themselves.

They become defined by what they do in church, rather than by who they are. Then you hit a problem.

That happens not just in churches. It happens everywhere.

In church, you hit a crisis when it becomes not about how we are worshipping the body of Christ in the church. It becomes about how that person is having their needs met.

It's very difficult to challenge somebody who has worked themselves into that sort of position. I have a mantra that I tell people:

"There are two great gifts you can give a community. One is when a job needs doing, to do it and do it well.

"The second, which is the harder one, is when you stop doing a job, do so with good grace."

I know from personal experience what happened when I stopped being church warden at St. Nic's.

I had been church warden there for years, and I'd been deputy warden before that.

I walked in to the church I'd been going to for

17

nearly twenty years, and I didn't know where to sit.

The church warden sits at the door. But
I didn't any more.

After all that time, I had to find
a whole new way of being. It was really hard.

People came to me and said:

"What do you want us to do about this?"

I said: "Well, I think you need to ask the church
warden."

Then the church warden came and said:

"Barbara, what do you think we should do about
this?"

I was fine saying: "These are your options",
because that was part of being there, to support
them. But I wasn't prepared to 'be' the church warden.

When I came here the church had been through a difficult time and it was kept going by people who were just determined that it was going to carry on.

Inevitably, there were those among them who had found their own niche.

But that very determination had led some people to build fortresses around who they were, or what they did. They just couldn't adjust to not doing things.

I get it completely. It was really difficult for me at St. Nic's. I was bereft. I'd lost a part of who I was.

I have great compassion and care for people who are in that position.

Sometimes not doing – just being – is much harder than doing, because you are far more vulnerable.

Mine is a very public profession.

We're the only ones left with this kind of role.

Previously in communities, the doctor, the school teacher, the policeman and the rector all lived in a 'house' – there was The School House, The Police House, The Doctor's House and The Rectory.

The people in these professions were the pillars of the community. They were there – they lived it, and they walked the streets.

The only people who still keep to that model of living are us.

I chose to come to this parish because I saw that here, the place of the parish priest is being able to walk about the parish. That is really what I am called to do.

It is a very public ministry.

Dog No. 3

Suki　　　**September 2006**

Suki is the only girl that I have had. She was a retriever/German shepherd cross.

She was prone to being sore where her belly folded (she was so slim). Each morning, I would wipe her tummy with a baby wipe and rub in some nappy cream to protect her skin.

The day came when she stole the tub of nappy cream and ate it while I was out.

When I came back she was sick all over the place. This was to be expected, but in this case the puppy sick was waterproof and impossible to clean up.

Suki

Chapter 4

The thing about a public ministry is how you take time off.

I define 'time off' as when I am in a place where nobody calls me Rector.

The other night I went for a ladies' 'pamper evening' with two of my friends who have been my friends since before I was ordained. So that was 'time off'.

But the lines blur. If somebody from church pops round to see me for a chat, because they know if I'm having a day off, is that 'time off'?

I have genuine personal friendships made at church. I'm not a 'professional' friend. It's how you sort out the fact that you're a human being and you live your ministry.

To many people there is always that bit of me that is The Rector.

And that's reflected in how we are paid.

I'm not paid to do my job. I don't receive a salary.

I'm paid a 'stipend' so that I can do my job.

A stipend is a regular amount that I am paid so that I don't have to go to work to earn money. That frees me up to exercise my ministry.

If you receive a stipend, part of the deal is that you have to live in the clergy house provided for you.

I have to live here. I can't say:

"I'll live somewhere else and just bus in."

Receiving a stipend instead of a wage is an interesting distinction.

It raises the question of whether I'm employed or not.

They've changed the rules about that now. It had to go through the courts to be sorted out legally.

Technically, I'm not an employee.

Somebody once asked me if I came here with an agenda.

What they actually said was: "Is this what you expected to happen?"

The answer is:

"No. I didn't come with an agenda. I came to listen and to see what would happen."

The church here has come a long way. We have a growing congregation and a rich variety of services.

We have Messy Church and Common Ground, (see glossary) which represent the informal as well as the formal sides of worship.

People are doing a variety of jobs and being a part of things.

And structurally we've changed.

When I arrived it was two parishes.

I followed two people who were each rector of a separate parish.

You can't be a rector of two parishes because you have to live in the parish. So I was the priest-in-charge of two parishes, rather than the rector of a single parish.

Then boundary changes were made to merge the two parishes into one, and I became the rector of the new combined parish.

In the new parish we have two parish churches.

They both have church wardens, but we have a single Parochial Church Council and a single annual Parochial Church Meeting.

It saves an awful lot of duplication. It makes some things easier – like my expenses. How do I decide what proportion of my expenses relates to each parish?

I didn't come here saying:

"We've got to become a single parish."

I came saying:

"We're two parishes. How do we work together?"

I have to say, the congregations of both parish churches have been brilliant about the merger. We've done it without any people throwing their toys out of their pram.

It's just been a case of:

"Well, that's what we're going to do," and getting on with it.

Dog No. 4

Piper   **January 2008**

When Piper was brought to me there were two puppies in the van. At the front, a blond 'Andrex Special' weighing in at 3kg. Everyone oohed and aahed. At the back, 6kg of stomach, skin and attitude.

Piper had arrived.

They went to scan his microchip, but there was never any doubt that this character was going to be my next puppy.

Piper had bilateral elbow dysplasia, and was withdrawn from training at 7 months.

The vets at Guide Dogs operated to correct the deformity and he went on to live happily as a family pet.

Piper

Chapter 5

Our two parish churches are Holy Trinity and St. Patrick's.

They are very different in style. Each is beautiful in its own way. They are both old, but one much older than the other.

Holy Trinity is an early Victorian building. Some alterations were made to the interior in 1937. A new organ was installed and new church furniture.

When Holy Trinity was built, St. Patrick's was already 600 years old.

First records date back to 1216.

Substantial additions were made in the year 1390. St. Patrick's is a Grade II listed building.

The roof was replaced in the 19th century.

Obviously, over the years there had been various modernisations at St. Patrick's but nothing in recent years.

Quite a lot needed doing internally to bring it up to standard.

We've made some major changes.

There was a lot of pressure, with people saying:

"We need to do this, we need to do that."

We agreed we were not going to do anything until we knew what the big picture was.

There was no point in rewiring the church just because we could afford to do that job, then finding in six months' time we needed to spend a thousand pounds moving the sockets because we had put them in the wrong place.

So we spent a long time agreeing the overall vision as a church.

And when that vision was agreed, we needed to get architects' plans drawn up.

After that, we needed to get permissions to do all this work. Then, out of the blue, we received an unexpected legacy which meant we could do it all.

We sorted out the electric wiring; we sorted out the lighting; we put in hot water boilers so we can make coffee; we put in a sink so we can wash the pots when we've made the coffee; we put in kitchen units so we can store the coffee and the cups!

These practical things make a huge difference.

We installed a slightly raised dais across the front of the nave. It has a wooden floor with a glass insert in it.

We have made a feature of the old alabaster tombstone beneath it by installing lighting so people can see it clearly.

We've moved things round to make a more efficient use of space.

The rector's vestry is now where the organ used to be. The former vestry is now used as a meeting room called Kay's room.

Kay is the lady who left us the money that paid for the improvements. The church is benefitting so much from them now.

Before I came there was a big hoo-hah about the organ going.

The organ had been there for over a hundred years. It went because it was beyond economic repair.

It never was a church organ – it was a house organ. It was never properly heard because the pipes were the wrong way round.

It was also quite difficult to play.

It was not in good condition so the decision was made to remove it.

Happily, we know somebody has got it who wanted it and appreciates it.

It went to a man who took it to an organ museum in Germany. There he reassembled and restored it and put it on display.

It was a hobby restoration on his part, so a labour of love.

We now have a computerised organ.

You would have to be an expert to know that it is not a pipe organ.

It's easier to play and it takes up less space – and it stays in tune.

Dog No. 5

Zorro   August 2008

Zorro loved going out for a run in the park. His enthusiasm was clear as he strutted his stuff around the place. When he was called back, he responded with equal enthusiasm.

However, he always had a bit of a braking problem, and would grin at you as he overshot and ran past, trying to stop. He came back as soon as he slowed down enough.

His other great joy when walking in the park was finding sticks to carry about – the bigger, the better. One day he was deeply frustrated because no matter how hard he pulled, this large stick was not moving. He didn't understand that it wasn't going to budge; the stick was still attached to the tree.

Zorro

Chapter 6

We also have a big improvement project on hand at Holy Trinity.

It was on the cards before I came.

There are records of an annual Parochial Church Meeting where it was said the choir vestry is falling down the hill and isn't safe.

Also the church hall needed a lot of work doing on it. I was surprised it was still standing.

So I came knowing that something must be done. Again, we spent a lot of time talking to people about what they wanted.

We talked to the Diocesan Advisory Council for the Care of Churches.

We said:

"What can we do with what we have?"

We ticked off the easy things that needed doing straight away. Then we had to look at the big picture.

Basically, it isn't economical to run a great big space and just use it for an hour a week for a service.

At the same time, we can't afford to replace the church hall, which is well used by numerous different groups.

So we've finished up with this huge building project to deal with both issues.

It will make the church a community space as well as a church space.

I think that when this project comes off, people will just love the result. It will secure the future of the church and improve it.

The entrance to the church land at present is right on the corner of the main road. Our plan is to move the entrance up the hill.

We want to use the stones from the church hall to reinstate the corner. Then, as you drive into the town, the first thing you will see is a smart stone wall.

If we move the town's colourful boundary sign to that corner, it will make a proper 'gateway' to the town.

Change WILL happen.

We can either take the initiative to choose what the change is, or we just let it happen to us.

I never came here to do buildings!

But it seems my ministry here is incidentally to sort out the buildings – to try and weave the church into the community.

The church needs to be there at significant points in people's lives. That's not just funerals and baptisms.

I'll have a conversation with somebody as I'm walking round the supermarket about something significant that has happened to them.

Perhaps they've just moved house, or got a new job, or whatever.

There is something about them being able to go to 'the church' and say: "I've got a new job!"

And whether they think of me as 'the church' or not, that has happened.

Our Christian faith is part and parcel of who and what we are as British people, because it has shaped so much of our ethos and our culture.

To weave that back into society, I think is
a great gift and a great honour. And that's what I'm
doing here.

And as to what's going to happen next – I've
got no idea!

I've not got any plans to leave, but the moment
will come when it will be time to go. I hope I have the
wisdom and grace to do that well.

There will be a point where the gifts that I bring
to this ministry are no longer what this place needs.

That might be when all the reorganisation has
been done. Or it might not.

But there's going to be a point where I've
worked myself out of a job because what this place
needs is a different shaped ministry.

But I don't know when that will be and I've no
plans to try to engineer it.

I shall be here until God tells me otherwise.

Dog No. 6

Erwin   **August 2008**

I thought Erwin was a great name
for a dog. That was until after I had
visited a local school with the new
puppy.

A parent told me her child had
come home from school that day and
when asked the puppy's name, the child
reported it as 'Urine'.

Erwin kept strict bedtimes and
loved a lie-in.

His eventual owner provided
him with a comfy bed by the radiator
in the office where he worked. He was
also remarkable for his ability to smile.

Erwin

Chapter 7

My route to becoming a priest was not a very straightforward one.

It was something I would always have loved to have done, but when I was at school it didn't exist as a career choice. Women were simply not accepted as priests in the Church of England.

Eventually, it did seem that it might be possible for me to follow that path. Even then, there were an awful lot of setbacks before I achieved my goal.

I had a very happy and settled child-hood in rural Nottinghamshire.

I went to a church school and attended our local

parish church with my family. My faith was always important to me.

I did well at secondary school. I passed all my exams with flying colours and went off to university to do a degree in theology.

For various reasons I had a very unhappy time at university and left after two years without completing my degree.

Of the available job options at the time the best one seemed to be accountancy. I did it without any particular difficulty but without any great relish either. It was a job.

As I said, my faith was always very important to me, and from then on, three strands of my life meshed – the church, my job and studying.

I became a church warden. I was a regular attender at St. Nicholas' parish church in Nottingham's city centre. It's known to one and all as St. Nic's for short.

When slum housing was demolished in the 1960's, St. Nic's was left without any parishioners. Nowadays the congregation is drawn from all over the city, the suburbs, and both the universities.

When I became a church warden at St. Nic's I was already on the Deanery Synod and eventually I became its Lay Chair (see glossary). I was also on various committees.

There was a lot of work relating to the inner city and urban priority areas.

I enjoyed being involved with the other churches in the city.

Then it became apparent that there were some challenges concerning the leadership in the church. I could tell there was something going wrong because every time I asked one of the staff at St. Nic's how they were, they burst into tears!

So I chatted to people, and in the end I made a commitment.

I said:

"I don't know how I'm going to do it, but if the only way we can sort this out is for me to be in staff meetings on a Monday morning, then I will be in staff meetings on a Monday morning."

So, with that promise ringing in my ears, I was left wondering:

"How am I going to do that, then?"

The second strand of my life was my job.

By this time I had had a career change. One of the things I had really enjoyed in my accountancy training was the data processing. So I retrained to become a computer programmer.

I spent the first few weeks of the data processing course thinking "I'm not thick – I will be able to do this!" And when I'd got over that phase, it was great. I was a square peg in a square hole.

I eventually got a very good job in software development for a big international company.

Here, my work was global, covering most of mainland Europe, Australia, the United States and South Africa. I did a lot of travelling. And I loved it.

The day after I made that promise at St. Nic's, I was called in to see my manager at work to be told there was a project coming up that only I could manage. We talked about it and I said:

"I'll do it, but there is just one thing – I want every Monday morning off. I'll work my hours and more, but I won't work Monday mornings."

And they said:

"Okay."

So I was able to keep my promise to St. Nic's.

God's good like that, you know!

Dog No. 7

Nevis   July 2010

Nevis was, to all intents and purposes, the ideal puppy. He was intelligent and obedient. He learnt to open all the doors in the house and wanted to be where I was.

His only drawback was that he hated walking in front of me. He would never lead. However hard we tried, he was a follower.

He went from me to Support Dogs in Sheffield to be considered as a Buddy Dog to an autistic child.

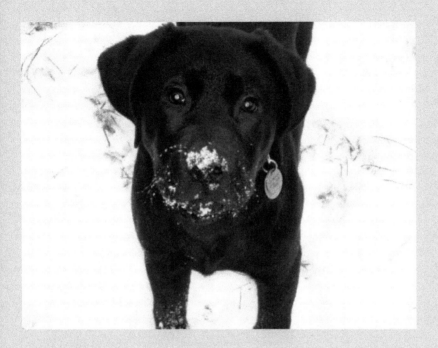

Nevis

Chapter 8

I knew I wanted to enter the ministry if I could.
I made several applications for ordination but I was
always told the time was not right. So, it was back to
the day job.

The first time I applied they said: "Not yet."
I left it a while and applied again. This time they said:
"No. You'll never be a priest."

So that was the end of that.

I couldn't understand why. I was thirty. I knew
that God had a call on my life. I just didn't know what
it was. Of course, I hadn't graduated because I hadn't
finished my degree at university.

I thought it would help if I had a degree of some sort, so I signed up for a part-time degree in business studies.

My employers were extremely helpful about adjusting my hours so that I could fit in my studies.

I eventually got my degree in business studies. My dissertation was a review of my employer's appraisal system, which went back to the company, so everyone got something out of it.

I settled down to being a church warden.

Then the Rector at St. Nic's announced he was leaving, and somebody said to me:

"Are you going to apply for his job?"

I said: "Ha-ha – of course not!" but inside me I knew that the answer was "YES" and that it was time to try again.

But I didn't do it straight away.

I talked to various people, members of the clergy I knew, and said: "What do you think?"

Everybody seemed to be saying it was the right thing to do. But the timing wasn't right.

It turned out to be a year before we filled the vacancy left by the rector. My Monday morning meetings carried on until we had appointed a new rector, so they didn't need me to be there anymore.

And the moment that happened, I was given a promotion in my job! That's been my experience all the time – if you give to God, you never lose out by doing that.

My fellow church warden had been church warden longer than I had. By the time we appointed the new rector he really wanted to stand down.

He felt he couldn't in the first year of the new rector's incumbency. He needed to be there in support. But after that he did stand down.

So there was one year of vacancy, one year with both church wardens being there for the new rector, and then, because my fellow church warden stood down, I stayed for another year. We couldn't both go together and leave the rector in the lurch.

So there were effectively three years of waiting before I started applying for ordination again.

I just needed to finish the job.

Dog No. 8

Bruno   June 2011

Bruno enjoyed going out for long walks with a group of us. However, he liked to know where everyone was.

Sometimes while we were out, one of the men would disappear behind a hedge.

Bruno was very aware that they had gone, and kept an eye out for where they were.

If you waited a couple of minutes then let him off the lead, he would rush off to find them and discover what exactly they were doing behind the hedge.

The yelps of surprise were rarely his!

Bruno

Chapter 9

So I went through the application process again.
As I was meeting the Diocesan Selection Panel,
a friend said to me:

"What do you want me to pray for, for you?"

"I want a yes or a no," I said.

What I got was a "Maybe".

So I went back to that person and said:

"I think you've got to learn how to pray
harder!"

The selection panel had said:

"You can come back in a year."

They set me to do some things during that time, which included a placement with a parish priest in a rural parish. Because I was at St. Nic's in the city centre, they assumed I didn't know anything about rural parishes. But I had grown up in one.

It worked well actually, riding shotgun for three months for somebody who had just come into a rural parish. It was a mutually very beneficial situation.

There had been a big scandal relating to the 'Nine O'Clock Service' in Sheffield (see glossary). Our diocese had a similar project running locally. Because of what happened in Sheffield the decision was very rightly taken that we needed to review this.

The diocese had several men on the review panel and they said:

"We could do with a lay person who is a woman."

They scratched their heads until somebody said: "Don't we know a church warden somewhere?"

So I got to do that project, which was wonderful because it was a really interesting piece of work.

The review panel reported to the bishop. So I got to meet the bishop. We had some very good conversations. And that review shaped my ministry here.

Because it was about how you do 'mission' when it's not done by going out and banging a tambourine in front of people.

It's about building friendships.

Also during that year I was invited to be Chair of the Governing Body of The Nottingham Emmanuel School, before they had any children enrolled.

There was a lot of work to do at that stage from designing uniforms to writing prospectuses – all sorts of things.

While I was doing that, my role changed in my day job.

I was redeployed within the company. For six weeks I had to turn up at the office but I had no work to do.

So I had time to do work for the school, such as visiting printers and talking to photographers. There was a lot of that kind of thing that needed to be done for the school.   I gave up the Chair of Governors position the day the school opened.

It was just at that point that I got another job.

By then I had done the year that the Diocesan Selection Panel for ordination had asked for.

I reapplied and was offered another selection day.

I started my new job on the Monday. I had my selection day on the Tuesday. On Thursday we were reporting on the 'Nine O'Clock' project for the bishop.

Quite a week.

The diocese accepted my application and I was on my way to a National Selection Panel.

At that selection panel, one interviewer asked me:

"What is truth, and how do you decide what is true?"

I said:

"I would go to scripture, and I would go to church history and tradition. That would be my starting point."

He looked at me with a twinkle in his eye.

"Would you burn heretics, then?" he asked. I smiled sweetly back and said:

"Yes, every November the fifth!"

Because that's what Guy Fawkes is based on –
burning Catholics.

At which point he burst out laughing and I was
accepted!

Dog No. 9

Gerry   **October 2012**

Gerry adored toys. At one puppy class, he ignored any lure of food or calling his name, as he had spotted the toy box. Once he had a toy, he was happy to return to me.

At home, he would find a toy and run over to where I was sitting, throw it in my lap and wait excitedly until I threw it for him, and then repeat the process again, and again, and again . . .

His excitement was so great he walked backwards, and so learnt to walk backwards on command — a great party trick.

Gerry

Chapter 10

Something interesting happened during the gap between the two selection boards.

The diocese wanted to start a link with another diocese. They were discussing who would go on the initial visit to see if the link would work.

They needed a laywoman under fifty, and the bishop invited me.

So I got involved in that very first visit to South Africa. I've been involved with the link with Natal, South Africa, ever since.

When I was thinking about my future life in the ministry, it was always my intention to be a self-supporting priest. I saw myself working for three days a week and being a vicar for three days.

Meantime, while I was studying I carried on working full-time and studied part-time.

People who were training full-time for the priesthood would be on a two year course.

There was an equivalent part-time course that took three years to complete. This course was offered to self-supporting priests.

The qualification at the end of both courses would be either a diploma or an MA, awarded by the East Midlands Ministry Training Course at Nottingham University. As I was going to be a self-supporting priest, I would be on the three year part-time course.

The bishop said:

"You don't need to do three years training. Just do two, but still part-time."

But the Director of Ordinands said:

"You've got to do the three years, so you should take the MA."

The principal of the college said:

"We'll compromise. Do the MA but do it in two years part-time," which is what I did.

I went straight into the second year.

That was a challenge, because the other students had all been together for a year. It was a question of where I fitted in.

Things did not start well. Twice in the first term we had a residential weekend.

At the first one, unfortunately I had a previous commitment which meant I got there late. It was 11 o'clock at night when I arrived. I had expected somebody to meet me, but nobody did, so I had to find my own way to my room.

I had been told that next morning there would be a meeting of my group, before breakfast. I turned up but there was no one else there! So it was all a bit of a nightmare.

At the second residential, our group was going to have a visit from the bishop.

Somebody had to be nominated to host the bishop when he arrived, so I was nominated as I knew him and we had been to Natal together.

In his talk, the bishop mentioned consecration, which is when someone is ordained as a bishop. He asked:

"Has any one ever been to a consecration?"

So I put my hand up, because I had. But nobody else did. And I thought: "Oops!"

The bishop said: "Oh, right. Whose consecration did you go to?" and I said: "Yours!" So that was funny.

And then somebody asked him a question about church schools and he hadn't got the numbers to hand so he said: "Barbara, how many church schools have we got?" I knew, so I told him.

Later that evening, when I walked into the bar, most of our group were sitting together.

Somebody said: "Oh, look, here's the bishop's pet!"

I think – I hope – it was meant in jest. Just bit of teasing.

They didn't know me from Adam. I'd missed a year and turned up from nowhere, the blue-eyed girl who can chat to the bishop.

I just looked at them and said: "Yes, but there's a difference between a pet and a poodle. I may be one, but I am not the other."

Dog No. 10

Zak   November 2013

  Zak was my tenth dog and first full German shepherd. He was a lovely caring dog, with such a kind face that toddlers would run up to hug him.

  His only drawback was that he did like to sing. We were once in a big service with people from all over the diocese. As we sang a hymn, he stood at the end of the row and joined in.

  The people from our congregation just took that for granted, but the row in front started giggling at him. The giggles started to ripple down the church, and I had to take him out before he disrupted everything.

Zak

Chapter 11

I was studying and still working long hours.
I was no longer church warden, because I had stood
down from that.

During the next year I gave up the Lay Chair of
the Diocesan Synod. But I was still on the Natal link
group.

I spent an interesting three months when the
link officer from Natal came over and I hosted him.

He stayed with some friends of mine. He
couldn't stay with me. That wouldn't have been
appropriate because I'm a single woman.

I arranged his programme. We travelled round

the diocese to all sorts of places.

I took him to deanery meetings and things like that, which was quite nice. He came on the residential training weekend with me as well. I really enjoyed his visit.

In the two years of my course I had just the one summer holiday. I went away for a couple of weeks, sailing.

While I was away I came to realise that I really should be looking for full-time work as a priest, not for part-time.

When I came back from holiday we began restructuring things at work.

I went to see my boss and asked him:

"Where do you see me in this restructure?"

He said:

"Well, the job that you do will be what you are doing now, plus the U.S.A. So one week in four you will fly to America."

Well, that was never going to work.

So I said:

"And if I don't want that job?"

He said:

"That would mean redundancy."

There were two of us up for that job and I was very happy for the other person to have it.

So I went through the whole of the restructuring process with nothing to lose.

I insisted people should be told the situation earlier rather than later. I made sure that nobody left without another job to go to.

I had time to work through the situation with them, how angry they felt, how rejected they felt.

So it was not the negative process that it could have been.

I went to the diocese and told them about my decision to become a full-time priest and asked how they felt about it.

The Director of Ordinands said:

"I'm glad you've realised at last."

I went to the bishop and he said:

"Jolly good!"

After you've completed your training and qualified, you do three or four years as a curate. It's like an apprenticeship, where you are an assistant and being trained to do the job.

I did my curacy in Chesterfield.

You're only allowed to apply for one parish at a time and they're only allowed to consider one curate at a time. So it's not a case of picking the best of three, or anything like that.

I applied to be a curate in Chesterfield which is in Derbyshire. I went to meet the people there and they accepted me.

I had always assumed that I would be ordained in Southwell Minster in the Diocese of Southwell and Nottingham. All the way through my journey the key points had happened in Nottinghamshire.

But Chesterfield is in Derby diocese so I would be ordained in Derby Cathedral.

While my company was still making redundancies, I finished all my university coursework. I got it down to a fine art. I could do a 5,000 word essay in a weekend.

My dissertation was completed and being bound when I moved up to Chesterfield at the end of May.

I had sorted out my house for letting.

Meanwhile, I was still working. So for a short time I commuted back and forth to the office in Nottingham.

I was awarded my degree in June. I was ordained on 4th July. I was officially made redundant two weeks later. And my redundancy pay cleared my mortgage!

So, God's been very good to me all the way through.

Dog No. 11

Lincoln   January 2015

Lincoln was a real livewire, he had no
off switch. His excitement at being anywhere
new was so great that when being carried
around as a tiny puppy he waved his paws in
the air. He soon worked out that the command
'wave' encouraged him to do this, and he
charmed people everywhere by waving on
command.

Only once did his energy falter.
A day trip to the seaside left him too tired to
walk so we had to take time out at a coffee
shop. Even after a rest, he plodded along back
to the car – until he saw the beach. Suddenly
all his energy returned as he tore round the
open sandy space and headed for the water.

Lincoln

Chapter 12

After I had been ordained I moved to
Chesterfield in Derbyshire, which left Nottinghamshire
looking for a new link officer with Natal. The new link
officer who was chosen was my spiritual director.

We had an interesting relationship going on
because whenever I came to see him for spiritual
direction, we always spent some time talking about
how things were going with Natal.

He was due to retire in the April as I came back
to Nottinghamshire in the February. Bishop George
asked me if I would take over as link officer. It was
always on the cards that that could happen, and
I am so pleased it did. It's a joy.

It's lovely because it's really challenging to see how other people live their faith in a different context.

It's challenging because you get to ask searching questions, like: "How much of the way I live out my faith is because of where I live rather than what I believe?"

It's quite often the things we take for granted that pull me up short.

For example, here in the Church of England, within the established church, I am rector of this parish.

The meaning of that is deeply understood in our national psyche.

It means I'm the local rector – your rector – whether you come to church or not.

But in Natal, the Anglican church serves the members of the Anglican church. So the sort of

question they have a discussion about is whether
somebody has the right to be buried in their
churchyard.

We would never need to discuss that. It simply
goes by geography. If your address is in the parish,
you have a right to ask me – your rector – to take
your funeral.

It's things like that we never need to question.
In Natal we had conversations where it took me
a while for the penny to drop.

I would say:

"Well, my parish has got a population of about
17,000 people",

And they would say:

"But how many of them come to church?"

Answer – about a 150 or 200. But they are all
my parishioners.

In Natal, they haven't worked out that the implication of having 17,000 parishioners is that I do a funeral a week, and conduct around 17 weddings or baptisms a year.

Because if they have a congregation of 200 people, they are the only people they do weddings and funerals and baptisms for. Here, by default, unless people choose to go to another church, I am the one.

The fall-back position is, if you want someone to be there, I'm the someone. People have a right to ask me, even if they are not an attending church member.

In fact, the only thing they don't have a right to do is come to the Annual Church Meeting. They do have a right to turn up and vote for their church warden, but not come to the annual meeting that follows.

It starts you thinking and you realise more about your own ministry.

I am proud to be Anglican when I consider that the Anglican church in Natal elected Desmond Tutu to be their archbishop.

1994 was the year when women began to be ordained in the U.K. In South Africa it was not until 1994 that citizens of all races were able to take part in democratic elections. Up until then even Bishop Desmond Tutu couldn't vote.

Some of the people I've met in South Africa, of every colour, have made life decisions based on their Christian belief.

There was a lovely white priest whose life was mapped out by the fact that everybody had to do national service. He didn't want to do national service because he didn't want to be ordered to shoot at his own people just because they were black.

So he opted to join the fire service, because the fire service would go and tackle fires wherever they were. It was colour-blind.

And because he joined the fire service he trained as a paramedic.

His whole life direction went with the fact that he had made that decision based on his faith and his ethics and his belief.

Sawley   February 2016

Sawley was a really special dog.
With his father due to retire, he has replaced
him in the breeding programme, so there will be
baby Sawleys around.

Sawley loved soft toys. He had
a particular preference for the large panda
that Sainsbury's was selling for Valentine's
Day. I was happy to buy one for him when they
were reduced after the day.

In the meantime, he would sit and bark
at the large box with the pandas in and try
to steal them from the display. He eventried
to help himself from other people's shopping
trolleys.

When he eventually got his panda home,
he would regularly fetch it and curl up against
it to go to sleep.

Sawley

Chapter 13

There is a real challenge in meeting people who were on the other side of apartheid.

I remember one lovely black priest pointing out to me:

"That's where my son goes to school." He was so proud that his son went to school.

He said:

"It's our future. Our hope. We can't get angry about what has gone before. Our hope is that my son will have an education."

It's just been a huge challenge to have talked

to these people. Their struggle isn't a theory, or something they've read about. It's their lives.

There is a lovely lady called Sue, whom I see regularly when I go over there. She wouldn't look out of place in a local Women's Institute meeting.

I first met her dressed in twinset and pearls. We were talking to her about the work she was doing with a group in Durban. We mentioned Christian Aid and the support they had received from them.

Then somebody asked her: "What about Amnesty International?" (see glossary). And this lovely lady replied:

"Oh, they were great. They always used to phone me half an hour before I was due to be arrested so I could tell my children where I would be in prison."

How could you meet people like that and not be awestruck?

That challenge is for us not to say: "Actually,

we've got it right in our western culture and we'll tell you how it should be done, and you'll thank us for it."

I've learned the humility of being challenged by others as well as challenging them. So you see the transformation that it has brought to me, and why I think it is important that we have these cross-cultural exchanges.

It's a big topic, and so much of what I saw was inspiring.

I shall cry when I tell you this, but I'll tell you anyway. On my very first visit we went to an AIDS hospice. At that time people were denying the reality of AIDS so they only actually got to the hospice when they had days left to live.

And we went and talked to the people there. They were all in beds. They had a men's dorm and a women's dorm with dividing doors. At the end of our visit they opened the dividing doors and said:

"Bishop, will you say a prayer of blessing?"

So he prayed with them. And a voice from one of the beds said:

"Thank you for coming, bishop." And the bishop replied:

"Thank you for letting me come. If I could, I would sing to you."

And one of the nurses said to the patients:

"Why don't you sing to the bishop?"

And so they did, even though they were in bed. They were tapping or moving their hands in time to the music. And they sang this song in their own language.

We asked:

"What does it mean?"

Even as they lay dying, they were singing about knowing the love of Jesus and that the cross was there and gave them hope.

I am still completely overcome when
I remember this. I can't help crying.

I came back home, and for weeks, as
I sat in church, these words came back to me, and
their singing came back to me and I just cried.

Eventually, several weeks later, I really heard
God saying to me:

"Why are you crying for people who died loving
me, and not for people who live not loving me?"

That's it, really.

Why was I crying for people who died knowing
about Jesus and his life-transforming gifts, and not for
the people who live without knowing that?

That's foundational to my ministry. People need
to know the love of God.

They need to know what it is to be truly loved because of who they are, not because of anything they have achieved.

And if I can do that in some small way, by God's grace, then I will do it.

That is why I am here.

Dog No. 13

Baggins   **August 2017**

Baggins by name . . . Baggins by
nature!

Even in his early months his character
is shining through. His first challenge is that he
throws toddler tantrums very loudly and people
who don't know him think he is very fierce. It's
just noise because he isn't ready to go to sleep
yet!

I am looking forward to knowing him as
a more mature dog who will be charming and
intelligent.

Baggins

Glossary

ADMINISTRATIVE AREAS – the Church of England divides the country into four administrative areas of ever-decreasing size.

Each area is in the charge of a priest.

The largest areas are in the charge of the most senior priests.

Each lesser sized area is in the charge of a less senior priest.

These are the four areas:

1 PROVINCE. Half the country, divided north and south.

2 DIOCESE. A large region within either of those two provinces.

3 DEANERY. A smaller district within a diocese.

4 PARISH. A local area within a deanery.

AMNESTY INTERNATIONAL – a worldwide non-governmental organisation focused on the human rights of all individuals.

ARCHBISHOP – the most senior rank of clergy.
There are only two archbishops, one in each half of the country. The more senior is the Archbishop of Canterbury (south); the other is the Archbishop of York (north).
Both archbishops sit in the House of Lords. They take a leading role in state ceremonials such as a coronation or a royal wedding.
An archbishop is sometimes also referred to as a primate.

BISHOP – a senior priest. There are 121 bishops who collectively have the responsibility of running the Church of England.
24 of the most senior bishops sit in the House of Lords and are involved in the law-making work of parliament.
Only a bishop can ordain another bishop, a priest or a deacon.

CHAPLAIN – a priest whose ministry is not carried out in a church, but who is attached to an institution such as a hospital, a school, a prison or the army.

CHARISMATIC – a form of the Christian church with these main characteristics:-
– judging between good and evil spirits;
– 'speaking in tongues' which means speaking an unknown, possibly mystical language;
– prophecy, which means receiving messages from God, including inspiration, visions and foreseeing future events;
– faith healing by means of prayers, gestures such as 'laying on of hands';
– strong religious belief.

CLERGY – ordained deacons, priests and bishops, in that ascending order of seniority.

CLERIC – the same as saying a member of the clergy.

CLERICAL COLLAR – a stiff collar worn by priests to indicate their role to people that they meet. The

collar fastens at the back. Sometimes it is worn so only a seamless white tab shows at the front.
It is jokingly referred to as a dog collar.

COMMON GROUND – 'Common Ground: Listening and Engagement' is a series of discussions within the Church of England about sexuality issues.
It offers different perspectives on biblical approaches to marriage and sexuality and provides an opportunity for questions and debate in an open-minded setting.

CHRISTIAN AID – An international charity working to alleviate global poverty regardless of the religion or race of those in need.

CURATE – a newly ordained priest.
A curate spends up to four years as an assistant to an established priest, somewhat like serving an apprenticeship.

DEACON – an ordained member of the clergy who is at the first stage of becoming a priest.
Deacons are permitted to perform some of the rites and rituals of the Church of England.

Many deacons move on to become ordained priests, but some remain deacons. They carry out their ministry in practical ways, caring for the sick, the dying, people in prison and people on the fringes of society.

DEAN – a senior priest, below a bishop.
A dean is the priest in charge at a cathedral.
A dean also chairs district committees (called Deanery Synods) within a diocese.

DEANERY – an administrative district within a diocese, which is run by a district committee of clergy and elected lay members.
There may be 20 deaneries within a diocese.

DIOCESE – a large administrative region run by a regional council (called a Diocesan Synod) under the oversight of a bishop.
There are 41 dioceses in the country.
Each diocese has a cathedral.

DOG COLLAR – a jokey term for a clerical collar.

ESTABLISHED CHURCH – a church recognised by law as the state church of a nation.

The head of state is the supreme governor of an established church.

EVANGELICAL – a form of the Christian church with these main characteristics:-

– being 'born again' as an adult;

– baptism by immersion in deep water;

– a direct personal relationship with God;

– believing in the authority of the Bible;

– spreading the Christian message.

EVANGELISE – to seek to convert people to Christianity

FAITH IN THE COMMUNITY – The 'Faith in the Community' report was launched in 2013. It was prepared by 'Christians in Parliament' and the 'Evangelical Alliance'.

The report addressed local authorities' fears that faith groups might offer services exclusively to people of their own faith, might be against equality, and may evangelise.

The report made recommendations to improve working relationships, and also highlighted the value of churches and other faith groups to local communities across Great Britain.

LAY – people who are very involved in the work of the church but have not been professionally trained or ordained.
Lay people are referred to in general as 'the laity'.

MESSY CHURCH – a form of Christian church with these main characteristics:-
– regular meetings;
– fun;
– family centred;
– creativity including 'messy' activities such as art and crafts;
– a shared meal.
These activities are intended for children and adults who are not normally churchgoers,

NINE O'CLOCK SERVICE – The Nine O'Clock Service was an alternative style of Christian worship for young people started in 1986 at a church in Sheffield.

The average age of worshippers was 24, mostly non-churchgoers.

Starting with ten people, the congregation grew to over six hundred.

In 1988 it was moved from the church to a large sports stadium in the city centre.

The Nine O'Clock Service was stopped in 1995 following a series of scandals that caused public shock and outrage.

ORDAIN – to perform a ceremony of consecration by which a person is made a priest.

Only a bishop can perform this ceremony.

ORDINAND – a person preparing to be ordained.

PARISH – the smallest, local administrative area within a district. This is in the charge of a parish priest based in a parish church, who may be assisted by one or more curates.

The parish is run by a Parochial Church Council comprising the priest or priests and elected lay members.

PARISHIONERS – all the people living within the parish area, not just the churchgoers.

PAROCHIAL – relating to a parish.

PRIEST – an ordained member of the clergy who has moved beyond the stage of being a deacon.
A priest is permitted to perform all the rites and rituals of the Church of England.

PRIMATE – the same as an archbishop.

PROVINCE – half the country, each run by an archbishop, Canterbury (south) and York (north).

RECTOR – a priest in charge of a parish or more than one parish.
Also sometimes called an incumbent.

SEE – another word for a diocese.

ST. NIC'S – St. Nicholas' parish church is located in Nottingham city centre.

St. Nic's is an evangelical, charismatic church. Silent worship is also highly valued, as well as practical action against social deprivation.

STIPEND – a regular amount of money allocated by the church to a rector to cover their living expenses. Being a rector is not a paid job. The stipend is to enable the rector to concentrate on their ministry full-time and not have to worry about earning money.

SYNOD – the church's term for a committee or council. A synod is made up of priests and elected lay members.

The use of several different colours of paper is unique to Dayglo Books. In total there are 6 tints, each in 5 levels of saturation, beginning with 'Very Light'.

This chart identifies the tints featured in this book. These tints are 'Light' which is the second level of colour saturation.

Coloured paper is known to be helpful in addressing problems associated with visual stress and dyslexia.

Blue	Hyacinth	
Cream	Banana	
Pink	Cherry Blossom	
Yellow	Pineapple	
Grey	Pebble	
Green	Jade	

Ingram Content Group UK Ltd.
Milton Keynes UK
UKHW050651280323
419284UK00008B/50